First Facts®

PRO WRESTLING SUPERSTARS

THE MIZ

PRO WRESTLING SUPERSTAR

by Matt Doeden

Consultant: Mike Johnson, writer
PWInsider.com

CAPSTONE PRESS
a capstone imprint

First Facts are published by Capstone Press,
1710 Roe Crest Drive, North Mankato, Minnesota 56003
www.capstonepub.com

Library of Congress Cataloging-in-Publication Data
Doeden, Matt.
The Miz : pro wrestling superstar / by Matt Doeden.
pages cm. — (First facts. pro wrestling superstars)
Includes bibliographical references and index.
Summary: "Introduces readers to pro wrestler the Miz, including his gimmick and
accomplishments in the ring"— Provided by publisher.
ISBN 978-1-4765-4208-9 (library binding)
ISBN 978-1-4765-6002-1 (ebook pdf)
1. Miz, 1980—Juvenile literature. 2. Wrestlers—United States—Biography—Juvenile literature.
I. Title.
GV1196.M59D64 2014
796.812092—dc23 [B]   2013032496

Editorial Credits
Mandy Robbins, editor; Ted Williams, designer; Jo Miller, photo researcher; Jennifer Walker,
production specialist

Photo Credits
Corbis: Retna Ltd./George Napolitano, 20; Getty Images: Bongarts/Joern Pollex, 18, WireImage/
Ron Galella, 10; Newscom: AdMedia/Byron Purvis, 9, Carlos Milanes, 6, WENN Photos/Carrie
Devorah, 13, WENN Photos/Jody Cortes, 15, ZUMA Press/Matt Roberts, cover, 17; Wikimedia:
Deron Kamisato, 5

Design Elements
Shutterstock: i3alda, locote, optimarc

Printed in the United States of America in North Mankato, Minnesota.
092013   007771CGS14

TABLE OF CONTENTS

MONEY IN THE BANK

World Wrestling Entertainment (WWE) champion Randy Orton was hurt and tired. He had just won a tough match. Suddenly, The Miz stormed into the ring. The Miz was carrying a Money in the Bank briefcase. The case gave him the right to challenge the champ at any time.

Money in the Bank Match

To win this match a wrestler must reach a suitcase hung above a ladder. The winner can challenge a title holder to wrestle at any time. The title holder can't refuse.

FACT

The Skull-Crushing Finale is The Miz's signature move. He grabs his opponent from behind. Then he smashes the opponent's face into the mat.

Orton had no choice but to face off with The Miz. The Miz attacked Orton's injured knee. The champ did his best to fight back. Orton tried a move called an RKO on The Miz. But The Miz reversed it! He grabbed Orton and put him in a move called the Skull-Crushing Finale. Orton was **pinned**. The Miz was the new WWE champ!

signature move—the move for which a wrestler is best known; often used to end a match

pin—when a wrestler is held firmly on his back for a certain length of time

THE EARLY YEARS

Michael Gregory Mizanin was born October 8, 1980, in Parma, Ohio. Mike loved sports, including pro wrestling. He was a good athlete. In high school, he played basketball and ran cross-country. Mike went to college at Miami University in Ohio.

FACT

Mike was an editor on the yearbook staff when he was in high school.

Mike with other members of *The Real World* cast

Mike's dream was to become an actor. In 2001 he joined the cast of the TV show *The Real World*. During filming the cast members were supposed to just be themselves. But Mike created a character for himself on the show. Whenever he got mad, he called himself "The Miz."

FACT

Mike also appeared on several seasons of the show *Real World/Road Rules Challenge*. In this show former cast members competed in various challenges against one another.

Mike thought that The Miz would make a great wrestling character. He attended a wrestling school and wrestled in small leagues. In 2004 he was picked to appear on the WWE wrestling reality TV show *Tough Enough*. He lost in the finals. But WWE officials were still impressed. They gave him a **contract**.

contract—a legal agreement between people stating the terms by which one will work for the other

WELCOME TO WWE

In the beginning The Miz worked mostly as a WWE announcer. He got to wrestle in 2006. He won his first match against Tatanka. The Miz was a **heel**. He called himself the Awesome One and made fun of his opponents. Fans booed every time he stepped into the ring. For a WWE heel, there was nothing better.

heel—a wrestler who acts as a villain in the ring

FACT

The Miz also wrestled under the name "The Calgary Kid." He wore a mask to hide his real identity.

The Miz quickly became a WWE star. He won two **tag team** titles with John Morrison in 2007. In 2009 he pinned Kofi Kingston to win the United States Championship. A year later he beat Randy Orton to win the WWE Championship.

tag team—when two wrestlers partner together against other teams

FACT

The Miz held the WWE title for six months. He called that period "The Era of Awesome."

Kofi Kingston leaps onto The Miz in a 2012 match.

The Miz won his next big title in July 2012. He pinned Christian to win the Intercontinental Championship. He lost the title to Kingston in October. The Miz surprised everyone by trying to shake Kingston's hand after the match. The popular heel was turning into a **babyface**!

THE TRIPLE CROWN

In 2012 The Miz earned the WWE Triple Crown. He held three major WWE titles. These were the WWE Championship, the Tag Team Championship, and the Intercontinental Championship. The Miz was the 25th wrestler ever to do that.

babyface—a wrestler who acts as a hero in the ring

THE FUTURE

What does the future hold for The Miz? His acting career is taking off. And whether he's a heel or a babyface, fans love him. It looks like The Miz has a bright future both in and out of the ring.

FACT
The Miz played the lead role in the 2013 film *The Marine 3: Homefront*.

TIMELINE

1980 – Michael Gregory Mizanin is born October 8, in Parma, Ohio.

2001 – Mizanin joins the cast of *The Real World.*

2004 – The Miz appears on the TV show *Tough Enough* and signs a contract with WWE.

2006 – The Miz wrestles in his first WWE match.

2007 – The Miz and John Morrison win two tag team titles.

2009 – The Miz defeats Kofi Kingston to win the United States Championship.

2010 – The Miz pins Randy Orton to become WWE champion.

2012 – The Miz wins the Intercontinental Championship. He becomes the 25th wrestler to earn the WWE Triple Crown.

2013 – The Miz stars in the action film *The Marine 3: Homefront.*

GLOSSARY

babyface (BAY-bee-fayss)—a wrestler who acts as a hero in the ring

contract (KAHN-trakt)—a legal agreement between people stating the terms by which one will work for the other

heel (HEEL)—a wrestler who acts as a villain in the ring

Money in the Bank (MUN-ee IN THE BANK)—a prize that a wrestler can use to challenge a title holder at any time

pin (PIN)—when a wrestler is held firmly on his back for a certain length of time

signature move (SIG-nuh-chur MOOV)—the move for which a wrestler is best known; often used to end a match

tag team (TAG TEEM)—when two wrestlers partner together against other teams

READ MORE

Brew, Jim. *The Miz.* Pro Wrestling Champions. Minneapolis: Bellwether Media, 2012.

West, Tracey. *Race to the Rumble.* Pick Your Path. New York: Grosset & Dunlap, 2011.

INTERNET SITES

FactHound offers a safe, fun way to find Internet sites related to this book. All of the sites on FactHound have been researched by our staff.

Here's all you do:

Visit *www.facthound.com*

Type in this code: 9781476542089

Super-cool stuff!

Check out projects, games and lots more at
www.capstonekids.com

INDEX